Blue Eyed Poet

Blue Eyed Poet
by Pramit Saha
Paperback Edition

First Published in 2023 by

Inkfeathers Publishing
Vivek Vihar, New Delhi 110095
www.inkfeathers.com

ISBN 978-81-19483-30-3

Blue Eyed Poet

Pramit Saha

Inkfeathers Publishing
www.inkfeathers.com

To all the blue-eyed poets, musicians, painters and artists who inspire me every moment.

Author's Note

I hark back to those days when that kid played truant to find ecstasy in his self-made world where factors like societal bigotry never harrowed him, as his world was sovereign—unfastened from this earth. In the bloom of dandelions, he played the violin, the gun of conundrums shooting bullets of realism, too, was unloaded. In fact, poets didn't die of hunger, painters never committed suicide, and dreamers didn't live by the gutter. But you know, as you grow up, you've got to face the music; you've got to cry for the moon to see a starry night idiosyncratically, as seen by Van Gogh. Life well-nigh stands a loaded gun—as if it is Dickinson's poem.

Poetry was not a bolt from the blue in my life; it took birth. It emanated inside of me in those evenings when my uncle recited umpteen pieces of poetry composed by 'unnamed poets'—neither did I comprehend surrealism, imageries, absurdities, or metaphors beneath those inscriptions, nor could I call to mind their names—I was just fifteen. But what exuded in me was 'a deep appreciation of art', the purity in impurity, death in life and life in death, peace in chaos and chaos in peace with uncle's room being a complete muddle—his paintings on paper slowly demolished by bugs, dust-stacked books scattered all over the place and bottles of rum sometimes whiskey tucked away underneath his bed.

In a song, my prophet, Bob Dylan, says, 'I met one man who was wounded in love, I met another man who was wounded in hatred'—The revelation of art rests in these wounds; that is my inference. The title of this book, 'Blue-Eyed Poet,' educes its inspiration from the 'blue-eyed son' of that song, who apprehends the contrast of myriad events of human life as a snowball effect for the hard rains to fall. I believe the journey of discovering this revelation is a pilgrimage where the saint and the devil together serve for the 'greater truth', which is not warped, rather it's a rare bird only seen by the drowning man who is strangled by emotions, contrasts, reality when he carves out an exquisite rhapsody from his blues, and that's his 'raison d'être'.

Remember, I just said you've got to face the music when you grow up! Well, you've to—especially when you're searching for the revelation of art, which is a bummock—wander like a gypsy! Certainly, the walls will yell that poets bring nothing but loneliness, anxiety and poverty to their families, but I want to translate a line from a Bengali poem by Himel Hasan which goes, 'Poet is a bleeding, independent, sovereign race of Almighty, don't ask why he's not a common man'.

About the Author

Pramit Saha is an emerging poet and musician based in Calcutta, with roots tracing back to the serene town of Tamluk in West Bengal. From a tender age, Pramit displayed a natural affinity for expression, his words flowing effortlessly onto paper. However, it was the world of music that initially captivated him. He was in kindergarten, when his mother taught him first four lines of one of Tagore's songs on harmonium which he performed at the annual function of his school and set the ball rolling. He became a student of music and started taking his vocal training and loved to play violin in his school. He delved into melodies and harmonies, weaving his artistic pursuits into a symphony of creativity.

It was at the age of fifteen that Pramit's poetic voice began to flourish, allowing him to explore the depth of emotions and experiences through his verses. A transformative encounter with the music of Bob Dylan reshaped his artistic ideology, catalysing the fusion of music and poetry into a singular, powerful force.

Pramit inherited both art and commerce as his genetic traits. In academics, he has just completed his graduation in the field of commerce but his dedication to his craft shines through as he continues to compose his distinctive blend of music and poetry being a learner simultaneously. Beyond the pages, Pramit is an avid reader and a compassionate listener drawing inspiration from the works of literary luminaries such as Emily Dickinson, Jibanananda Das and Fyodor Dostoevsky as well as musical legends like Bob Dylan, Leonard Cohen, Pink Floyd, B.B. King, Frank Sinatra and many more. Pramit's creative spirit is further ignited by the artistry of Vincent Van Gogh along with his letters to Theo leaving a deep imprint on Pramit's youth.

As you traverse the tapestry of Pramit's creations, you'll find yourself immersed in a world where words and music intertwine, igniting the senses and resonating long after the final note is played.

Heroin

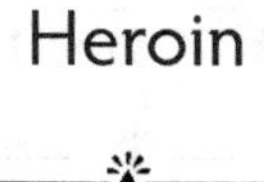

Glaciers float in the depth of eyes,

Outside is painted white,

Agonising love injects heroin

Into some moments of warmth

Traffic Signals

Pain has a body, probably a face too,

Expressions of despair are bulged-out tumours,

Mere oblivion is a friend of the night,

Perception of this world moves in between traffic signals.

Autumn

Autumn will arrive in your sleep,

Friends who were leaves—left for their destiny,

All alone in bed—the body hides a tree,

Birds will come back in spring.

Dot

You and I were born from a dot,

It was ink with which our eyes were drawn,

The depth of colour absorbed sunlight

For an evening to descend from our love.

Like A Wildfire…

Like a wildfire, it rages out—

Everyone rushes for their own lives,

Time is burnt down—as if a corpse,

April showers wash it all away

Toys

Never-ending pain is quieter than whispers—

More dangerous than stretching arms like birds,

Objects at a distance appear as toys

To a child who crawls like the setting sun.

Afternoon Light

Afternoon light digs its grave in a sweater,
An evening mourns with mists,
Wild winds disguised as cold breath—
Long for that woman in bed.

High Tides

All I can see is white wilderness,
A sound echoes from both sides,
Eyes—pitch dark—which engulfed high tides
Loses everything in sweet tenderness.

Her - I

Her hair covers the mountains,

I stand and wait for her grace,

Breath travels from valleys

To touch her river face,

Our unholy pride slanders the radiant sun,

Wildflowers are the lovers of rain,

I still stand and wait for her grace

Until an enigmatic sky becomes golden.

Lullaby

Grief in my heart isn't a frontman,

The sweet child doesn't sleep without her mother,

Voice trembles when eyes don't find vibrant colours,

Lullaby resembles a melancholy—

Sound

Sonic vibrations are exchanged in dialects

To measure love in decibels,

A sound is entangled with a picture—

Like the moon is entangled with smoke.

Daffodils

How this fire rages from earth
And burns the daffodils alive,
A painter has to dive—
In yellow for their rebirth

Meaningless Life

Meaningless life stands still,

Eat that flesh of your prey like a carnivore,

Blood dripping from the mouth has a taste,

Feelings penetrate your mind for an explosion—

Black and white piano conceals a rainbow.

My Dear

It ends with a smile from behind those eyelashes—

I saw you waving at me—my dear—

Our words were orphans in the streets

When fragrance slowly died…

Flower Girl

A droplet of rain traps itself in a glass—

To live as a memory,

The sight of a funeral comes and goes—

As the clouds turn grey,

A sound gives birth to other sounds—

And makes harmony,

The flower girl leaves her favourite flowers behind.

Classroom

Boards and walls are scribbled,

Plants have grown on waterlogged minds,

I'm in the middle of a wave—

Seagulls are flying over me.

Horizon

Living for a moment was a choice
The dead never took,
A song for the newborn
Brings sleep as a gift,
As old as a year gets–
Nerves become crossways,
Involute as it is, a traveller
Never reaches the horizon.

Under the Light

Live a lie before living a truth,

Unless you're under the light

Viewers can't see you,

As time passes, colours will fade away from this dress

Look for the light at that time.

Waltz

Sound of birds changed,

No one knew whose eyes had first seen the moon,

Noir tone of the roof voiced solidarity with night,

Lovers did kiss when they danced the waltz

Where darkness was a shallower shade of watercolour

Jasmine

When the sun sets, everything around gets colder,

We've to dig deeper into each other—

'Til we smell Jasmine,

Denser the forest—sweeter the pain,

Every breath feels like a hot breeze on the glacier,

Incessant streams are flowing like drum beats—

Gale

Outgrown green fields never ended

But the steps did,

A twilight dissolved in dark blue iris

Once witnessed a choir of birds—united—

In the wake of gale—

Home

Meagre conversation loses vapour,

Sound of footsteps slowly fades

Leaving the past in asylum,

The child has lost his way home

Her - II

Her eyes looked out for the clouds,

Her chariot was waiting for her,

When lights engulfed the sound—

Dawn broke out on her bed.

Distant Worlds

Some feelings become wounds—

Numbness is a dying light,

A flower on the coffin leaves love alone

Which never meant to travel distant worlds.

Ignorance

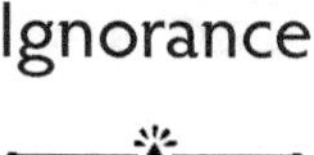

The door closes every time

When evening bells are heard,

The waiting time loses devotion and its worth,

There are crows feeding on dead

And fire lighting up cigarettes,

Ignorance helps the blind to live…

Carriage

The carriage has arrived again to take somebody,

Smell of rotten meals has taken over the room,

A mother, a father, a brother locked the door to resist,

In no time, the ashes looked for sunlight—

Stairs

I was soaked up in dirt,

Everyone had seen my fall, but no one saw me,

That earthly pleasure didn't stay long

For the stairs were mountainous–

I had to climb until I reached the falling point.

Pandemic

It itches when the body touches poison,

Feelings are suffocated—throat being pressed even tighter,

At this moment, diseases spread like pandemic—

People hide their skeletons with flowers.

Emptiness

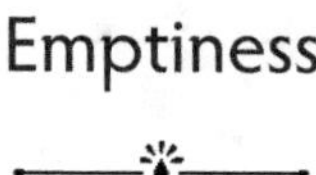

Borders evanesce in the dark—

Chasing eyes pause for a moment—

Where does it all go—

The colour—the scent—the love—a lover—

Deep-inside absorption becomes a long procedure

To feel emptiness with an empty heart

Suicide Note

That bloody bullet was a friend

To take away the pain—

The sky was red-hell,

Walls of the room—

Listening to sounds of silence,

The moment your eyes closed

You got teleported to the life you wanted,

Existence was a washable stain.

Paradise

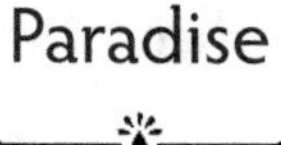

You had to change something

Before this place was left deserted,

Many may have passed purgatory now,

While they wait for their acquaintances

The paradise remains unknown

Her - III

When a song comes to an end–

A solid body breaks down into fragments

And disappears in this lonesome universe,

With my bare hands—

I keep trying to touch her—darkness

Glass Prism

My body was given to me—

Just like my name,

Destiny itself creates and breaks realities,

An atom is as capable as the strongest creature,

At the right time, every element will disperse like light.

Bus Ride

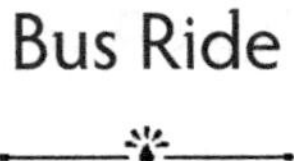

Heavens may disdain the suffering—

The damned took at the eleventh hour,

Glance at life from a bus ride highlighted

Rancour of a fellow traveller for his austere life.

Necklace

How long life's gonna wait

If thunderstorms pass and hail follows through,

Sing some lines in your trembling voice—

Let fear hang like a necklace…

Break

I saw the universe in a stranger's eyes

Where heavens and stars collided,

As lips trembled to find the sun—

The planets revolved around

Waiting for a new form of life to begin

Wishes

Some of my wishes are kept for the next life,

When I drown—I'll remember your love,

The opera would sing in chorus,

Slow and steady audience would cry for tragedy—

Hope

When hope ushers a slanted light to the skin pores—

Dawn steps in through the door,

Like soundless words—bodiless love—

There're only spaces in between,

A minute passes, but shadows stay still—

Sleeping Beauty

I can't sleep after seeing the sleeping beauty,
Flowers like arrows pierced her skin
To form a garden,
The sound which awakes this world
Doesn't wake her,
Dust takes all her beauty away

My House

My house burns down like paper,

Flowers grow on the gentle ruins,

Ambulance rescued the wounded

While rains have rescued the dead.

Civilization

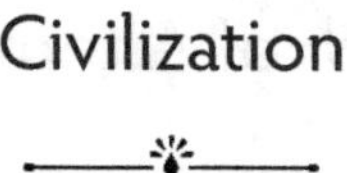

Cracks on the concrete showed—
Birds had left their lifelong abode,
Through nerves and branches, solitude crowed,
I only left a word for the road,

Civilization laid on a side—
Naked–waiting for the tide,
By the law of nature, sins had to abide—
Leaving the end open—wide—

Death of Afternoon

World has become void by losing its smell,
The length of the sky equals the length of a palm,
A painter tries to feel his painting only by touch
And an afternoon dies in his arms.

Name

I want to give this life a name—
Pure but a mispronounced chant,
The mystery of birth and death awaits
Being discovered in the eyes of an infant,

A name used for the rovers
When they feel homesick,
The sky appears as concrete
In the hearts made of brick,

Liberation lures with delusional dreams—
Helpless is the slave's plea,
Moses, with his stick, stretches forth
To divide the red sea—

Falling

In this dream of mine–I'm falling—

Falling from the skyscrapers—

Falling from the mountains–to the darker world,

Darkness doesn't let you see what's inside,

Sooner or later, you'll be a part of it.

Tsunami

At times it's blue all over the place,

Tyranny separates my mind and heart

For the tsunami—to take away both,

Fantasies about a naked night

Do not let me sleep.

Almighty

The bird wanted to fly—
Higher than the clouds—
Higher than the aeroplanes,
A height from where
The ocean looked like a string of pearls,
In a vacuum where
Countenance of the almighty could be spotted,
His loneliness could be felt—

Greyish Mind

That night when nobody was around,
A feeling for the sky was found—in my heart
A storm was raging
And warmth felt oceans apart,

Some hours did pass by,
That feeling had to die—leaving behind
Morning rains
In my greyish mind.

Her - IV

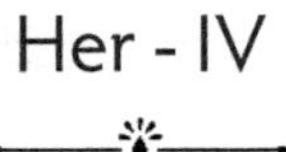

My deepest secrets are too lonely,

When the sky will be covered in a pinkish hue—

I'll tell her,

Sound of sailing ships would bypass crimson-red walls,

I cannot refuse when the sea calls—

Belongings

Our belongings have materialistic values—

Attached to this earth—with care,

The estranged children of affection—

Have to grow in survival

When their abode is sold.

Continuity

Cold-blooded cowards handed over the honour
To admirers of black and white,
A sapling—too young to inveigh
Stood silent in broiling daylight,

The stronger gets the doze—
Effete efforts extol beauty,
A soldier buried in silence
Is lost in the continuity.

Majesty

In the absence of innocence—

A priest sleeps in superstition,

Beneath God's eyes

Connivance has conquered the kingdom,

Servants bend down on their knees—

For Majesty's mercy.

Escape

Confusing is the way
To find an escape,
A stone heading into the abyss—
Never comes back to the surface,
A feather meant to bring hope—
Is dislocated in opaque wilderness

Lustre

Deep in the chambers
A man hides from the moon,
Lust howls as a wolf—
Exposed to seclusion—
Afraid of losing lustre.

Charade

There lies pride

In the embers—

Left behind to remember—

The only truth is a charade—

Passed from our ancestors

In a posh tradition.

Romance

In inflated silence

These walls breathe heavily,

Insomniac thoughts kill romance—

Intense but scared of

An empathy-less life

Edifice

The weight—unfathomable—

An edifice erected over feeble

As a memorial citing the triumph—

A champion's potential—

Unwilling to share a crumb.

Kaleidoscope

Through marble eyes

Look into this kaleidoscope,

Valleys of mirages—mountains of illusions—

Deserts of dead and cursed conurbations

Symbolise handcuffs and chains,

This reality is cramped—

One more poem would not fit—

Bitter Sensation

Clumsy these words

Trigger a bitter sensation—

A bitter taste—

Every mouth hurls with hostility

To hearts—estranged—

And stab to death.

Her - V

Dressed in formal attire—

Perfume of rain-drenched earth—

Serenity on carpets—

A bed of lavender—

Arrangements made to welcome

Leaving aside ruth of living,

To sing a song for her—

When she arrives

Maelstrom

A maelstrom engulfs

Sanity, society, aphorisms, animus—

To baptise them

Or be their watery grave—

Just for the spirit's sovereignty.

Private Life

The dagger waits to slit a throat–incapable of moaning,

Every drop of blood gets lost in the Pacific,

Art is nothing more than an orgasm—

Felt in your most private life.

www.ingramcontent.com/pod-product-compliance
Lightning Source LLC
La Vergne TN
LVHW050337160826
845677LV00014B/3649

* 9 7 8 8 1 1 9 4 8 3 3 0 3 *